INSIDE THE BRIGHTNESS OF RED

First published 2010
by Second Light Publications
9 Greendale Close
London SE22 8TG
www.secondlightlive.co.uk

ISBN: 978-0-9546934-8-0

British Library Cataloguing-in-Publication Data
A catalogue record for this book is available from the British Library.

Printed by CPI Anthony Rowe
Cover design: original artwork by Martin Parker
Designed by Martin Parker at www.silbercow.co.uk

Also by Mary MacRae
As Birds Do
(Second Light Publications, 2007)

Mary MacRae

Inside the Brightness of Red

It is this great absence
  that is like a presence, that compels
    me to address it without hope
of a reply....

RS THOMAS

Second Light Publications

PREFACE

Mary MacRae died in July 2009. She was 67 and had written poetry for a little over 10 years. She had published one collection, *As Birds Do* (Second Light Publications, 2007). She also left behind a body of work which had not been published in book form, from which Myra Schneider and Dilys Wood have made this comprehensive selection. The poems are arranged thematically in sections, each of which is intended to show a particular aspect of Mary's work.

I and others believe that Mary's lyric gifts deserve to be more widely known. Her family and I are grateful to Myra Schneider and Dilys Wood for their help in making this possible and to Mimi Khalvati for her afterword.

Lachlan MacRae

ACKNOWLEDGEMENTS

Some of these poems or versions of them have appeared in *ARTEMISpoetry, Brittle Star, The Interpreter's House, Long Poem Magazine, Magma, Murray Street, Quattrocento* and *Scintilla*.

CONTENTS

DAFFODILS

Wild, just hatched,
flinging yourselves out
dampish

after breakthrough,
papery halos intact
at the spring of the petals,

grey-stemmed Lent Lilies
so interleaved with light
we can't pin you down,

unearthly,
and ready for your ascension
weeks ago

but attendant,
waiting for us somewhere in the wings
like angels,

your darting after-image
between the pear-tree
and the brick wall.

WINTER SUN

Again the cyclamen, its flowers ever more white
as they edge slowly towards violet

each single petal
finely creased like a miniature fan;

together they form funnels where sunlight congregates
then splashes on to the glassy stems.

WHITE

You can disappear in a house where
       you feel at home; the rooms are spaces
for day-dreams, maps of an interior
       turned inside out. See, you turn your face

from the light, and the white room crowds in,
       part beckoning to other places
through the odd angles of half-open

door and window, partly enfolding,
       with the radiator's soft-pressed pleats
and chalky marble fireplace holding
       even the tablecloth poised in neat

suspension. You bend to the cat's purr;
       become the pattern of light and heat
blown in with the garden-scented air.

At the table, you stir your coffee.
       The quiet of the house flows through you;
you dream its dream while the hanging tree,
       the yellow rose bush and the deep blue

of thunder-struck hills imprint themselves
       on chairback, cup, blouse. Across the room
a man looks at you and sees himself

framed on the opposite wall in gold,
       his mirror-image gathering the light
to a glowing backdrop. You still hold
       your spoon and the big coffee bowl, white

against the white cloth, watch the milky
        bubbles trail their slipstream spirals right
to the rim, collapsing with a sigh.

You know the blossom's out when the light
        turns thick. It flows from the almond tree
into the room, faintest pink on white
        like sweet almond milk, an ivory

coolness that washes you of colour.
        You bathe in its scent, its January
facing-both-ways-ness, and remember

the soft green of the nutshell's velvet.
        You've had too much yellow and crimson;
better to be bleached and faded. Let
        it all go; soon the door of your room

will be locked, leaving only a slight
        hint of you still, a ghostly perfume
lingering in threadbare curtains and sheets.

ELDER

A breathing space:
the house expands around me,

unfolds elastic lungs
drowsing me back

to other times and rooms
where I've sat alone

writing, as I do now,
when syncope –

one two three one two –
breaks in;

birdcall's stained
the half-glazed door with colour,

enamelled the elder tree
whose ebony drops

hang in rich clusters
on shining scarlet stalks

while with one swift stab
the fresh-as-paint

starlings get to the heart
of the matter
              of matter

in a gulp of flesh
and clotted juice that leaves me

gasping for words transparent
as glass, as air.

YELLOW MARSH IRIS

It's how I imagine prayer must be
this looking and looking
at ten flower-heads of marsh iris
in a lipped glass vase

their stiff stems magnified
by water, criss-crossing
white, pale green, green
in a shadowy coolness

and the petals so yellow
they remind me of someone I loved
long ago – when she came in
it was like a light switching on –

as this sudden burst of sun
through the pavement tree
makes ripples run through the room
and the dust-specks dance

leaving only the flower-heads unmoved
in their poses carved out of air,
curled and stretched across
the shapes of negative space

while my eye flicks back and forth
tracing where the light catches
a darker tongue of gold
in the petals' centre

until they seem to hold
all words, all meaning,
and what I'm reading
is a selving, a creation.

KOREAN COLOURS

The gingko leaves are falling, small yellow
hearts, like love-letters slipped through a window,
and three girls scoop them up, laughing, throw
them over one another, snapping their cameras,
almost in the shadow of the Pagoda-with-No-Shadow.

And on the pavement in Gongju, old women snip
the stalks from chillies, sack after sack, sitting
all day in the icy wind, their shiny scissors
punching little holes in the conversation,
and warm their crabbed hands at the chillies' crimson.

POMEGRANATE

October: too cold for such flaunting,
such glimpses of bunched frill,

flounces of deep pink lace barely contained
in their waxy sheath,

such gorgeous gold tassels.
The buds are unabashed

straining their smooth sepals
towards breakthrough

too far north, too late.
Underneath,

in the tree's shadow
lie small puckered fruit,

black on black.
These pomegranates can't ripen –

won't open their caskets to show
twin embryos of glistening flesh,

red cells, skin,
tucked tight to the wall –

just stiff scuffed purses
and a few dry seeds.

HAUNTED

A blueish frost strokes the tousled grass
and the stars have turned to milk; sky hangs in folds,
a warm honey-combed quilt over my bed.
From the wood across the field an owl calls
and its cry comes shaking out in spiralling rings,
a lasso to take me back, a smooth cool cord
winding me round.

             I've never felt so safe
as in the rectory where my great-aunt lived
in Burton Bradstock. Haunted it may have been,
but by familiar ghosts. Along the wall
that ran right round the garden were tall trees –
I didn't know their name – with flattened branches
like green-black shelves. Pressed against the bricks
stood figs, with leaves like hands, and hanging fruit
I loved to touch, fingering the warm, soft flesh.
At night the owls sang for me, threw their skeins
of notes in long brown lines over the roof;
the dark was a feathered arch, filled with wings
and wing-beats, heart-beats fed into my pulse.

They drum there now, resonating strings,
lifelines to a gladly haunted past.

KÉRKYRA 1961

I'm full of power, nineteen and immortal.
We want for nothing. We sleep in the open air
under olive trees, and when we bathe at night

we're heroes clothed in silver phosphorescence.
Evenings, we make a fire of dry driftwood
and brew cocoa with the brackish spring-water

from the far end of the beach. The air's velvet,
fragrant with sea and land smells, the moon glitters.
Then from the steep hills, two princes come

with talk and laughter; there's no need of names.
Overhead there's an arch of constellations,
the same I saw at home, but wider here

where gods live among them. What matter, now,
if princes become old men or kings or exiles?
What matter if I look back down the years

and guilt and shame confront me? Entirely changed,
I'm still that girl, sometimes the fire burns on
and I feel its warmth, glad that it is so.

VILLANELLE

Papery ghost, why do you haunt me so?
You slip between my pages day and night;
I'm half angry, half afraid. Let me go.

Yours is the face against the dark window,
you conjure me in dreams, won't let me write.
Uneasy ghost, why do you haunt me so?

Who's in control? In sleep's dark undertow
we're swept away, cut off from the light
till I'm angry, half afraid; let me go.

What have you come to say? You miss me? No.
That's not your message. Yet, perhaps, you might.
Quiet ghost, why do you haunt me so?

You thread your life through mine and although
those silky spider strands are plaited tight
I'm still half afraid you'll let me go.

So late to visit. So much that you know
I want to ask. Silent, you smile. Goodnight,
familiar ghost; why do you haunt me so? –
don't be afraid I'll ever let you go.

BLOOD LINES

My first house has airy spaces
then you
running into the kitchen

with a bagful of squirms
to clang the bowl into the sink
and make the water ring like bells

as you tip the slithers in,
the whole lot at once,
a slippery silverskin knot.

They swim round and round slowly
in the chipped bowl
looking blue underwater, cold

and at home, blunt heads
pushing on through their small sea,
mouths like gashes.

You swish the water
but snatch your hand back quick, quick,
with a short word

and I see crimson strands
criss-crossing the silver
and you, sucking your finger

as you show me their needle teeth,
and in that sharp instant
I know you're my father.

JAPANESE ANEMONES

Peel back the outer layer (my thick adult
fingers fumbling and clumsy) and inside
each green bud there's a padded satin button. Stroke that hint
of silvery plush and remember
how the name can ripple and slide
on the tongue –

how these buds of Japanese Anemone
used to hold secrets I could creep into
and unfold right to their blue-grey hearts; I liked what I found.
'There'll be no flowers', you warned, but
there were always flowers and I knew
you were wrong.

Of all your late summer plants – frilled hollyhocks,
sweet peas in fine lawn, or the dahlias,
stiff and stand-offish, you tended with such care, rushing out
bare-headed into the hailstorm
to hold a large black umbrella
over them –

it was those anemones, leaning forward
as if about to speak, with their dense white
petals open to the sun, paper-flat, and gold stamens
fringing the green at the centre
until they curled inwards at night,
that I loved.

They weren't your favourites, but the ones under
my window seem like a memorial:
they spring up in the narrow cracks between the paving-stones
unasked, and make themselves at home
as if they're pushing through hard-core
to the heart.

HEADLONG

You never learnt to steer anything,
only fast-forward, dead straight. To reverse,
turn, look over your shoulder, had you baffled;

eyes front, foot down, you hurled your jeep
to the end of the war then cut out
those years with your clasp knife.

All subtraction was painful: home on leave
you'd be kit-bagged hours before your train,
your whole stay shadowed by going.

Once demobbed and in Civvy Street
Shanks was your pony, yet despite the drill
you couldn't keep in step or match your long stride

to her high-heeled pace, but sent her on ahead,
followed quick-march until you kept up,
arrived panting, together; kissed.

That's what you wanted: to know she was
just out of sight and you speeding towards her.
Later you broke rhythm – no-one to follow,

no-one you missed more than her – tried to right
your blurred vision, fill the gap
by emptying glass after glass.

Only at ease, then, in the garden, you coaxed green,
still sharp-eyed enough to root cuttings
you tamped with your clumsy fingers, gently.

Unsurprised at how quickly time passed
at the end, you hurried off, always in readiness,
leaving your familiar flowerpots half-planted,

the seedling strands high and dry, and in a last
headlong burst, surged, breathless,
straight forward with arms outstretched.

NOTES, 1967

My mother, then. Her last-minute lists,
not many, just the days things should be done –
Monday, dustbins, Tuesday, collars. A box –
I see it now – of riveted brown cardboard,

'Collars' written in boldly scrolled italic
on its lid. She must have thought of him
fitting the collars one inside the other,
five white rings, stiff as the box they went in,

leaving them on the step to be collected.
More lists, biro-written, tucked in beside
the breadbin on the dresser where we put
bits of paper we didn't want to lose.

My aunt asking if I thought he'd mind
if she washed the night things when he brought them back;
I didn't think so. How could I know, or care?
Later that afternoon I saw her nightdress

dripping on the concrete. Maybe it rained
but I don't remember that, or anything else
about the weather, just the mottled length
of cream satin hanging wet on the line.

Drowning inside someone else's coat,
borrowed and black – my own, new, close-fitting,
coral-red, he wouldn't let me wear.
Turning the collar up; so cold that day.

SYCAMORE

Shake the bright glass dome: snow starts to fall.
    Mother in a shapeless blue fur coat
is pouring tea into very small
        Japanese cups while flakes drift and float

past the sycamore. It's dusk; the light
    has all seeped into the snow. We've put
a cloth on the cucumber frame, white

on white ermine trim, and sit round perched
        on orange boxes. It's Christmas Day;
the cake is coal-dark and tastes as rich
        as flame. Ash-crumbs settle. Locked away

in ice, these remains thaw in the turn
    of a globe to show a grey tree where
Chinese Lanterns still rustle and burn.

VIRGIN AND CHILD

from the studio of Roger van der Weyden

With her right hand she holds the breast
between her fingers, pushing the nipple forward
and looks down, concentrated. The baby looks, too;
a blue vein throbs as the milk comes in.
And I feel again the warmth of the held child,
years past ovulation dream the vital second
when the sperm finds the egg, how they grow together
and swirl towards a safe harbour and silt to lodge in.

When I was a girl, the frost made ferns
on my window, their leaves spread over and over;
moss on a shady path was a firework star-burst.
What endlessness of variation: sand-ridges
made and unmade with every tide; all the unborn,
children and grandchildren, the womb unfulfilled.

UNBORN

I never really understood it. In the shadow
of Daisen's holy peak, little piles of stones,

cairns, on the dry river bed, hundreds of them, hundreds
to be swept down in the flow when the river was in spate,

each – I was told – a lost child, the pebbles chosen,
placed, one by one, with an empty sound,

small memorials
to the unborn.

So when a girl surfaced in my dream, half-drowned
and stretched out her hand, I thought of children –

all the ones I'd never had – as seed-pearls that hadn't caught
the light, washed away in their hundreds

and distant as the spread of stars that shone
borrowed gleams on my dark window.

LOOKING FOR A CHILD

True singing is a different breath, about
nothing. A gust inside the god. A wind.
Rainer Maria Rilke: *Third Sonnet to Orpheus*

Something withheld:
small dry flowers, juniper, blueberry
thin against the wind's edge, clouds
being built, packed, light unpicked

and the sun so low in the sky
that everything's at impossible angles,
the curve of the hill seeming to mesh
with the curve of her eye

so that all she can see is ridge and furrow,
with the wind like a voice
asking her to look and look
while it swells in her, a horror,

picturing a child under a hedge,
in a ditch, crouched in dead leaves,
and she's braced stiff against
this nameless cold, this blueness,

until the shadows shift –
dark petals blown on grass, dense
then scattered – as something
small in the narrow gateway

comes into focus slowly,
she feels light flood in,
enter her body like buoyancy
and she's breathing colour not air,

her lungs so easy there's no longer
this moment, that moment,
but being taken into the mechanism,
the smooth silent running,

disembodied, time spinning
on the spot, always now,
as she gathers the found child close
and speaks her name.

BITING HER NAILS

Newest of new moons, you're such a sliver this morning
in the pre-dawn blue, you remind me of fine parings

from the tip of a baby's finger, the eerily perfect nails
my new-born had all those years ago, like pink sea-shells

in miniature, already so long they needed cutting. The nurse
told me to bite them; safer, she said, than using scissors.

But holding flimsy fingers still wrinkled and filmed with wax
against my lips, trying to catch the nail in a half-bite, half-kiss

was ten-fold anguish for me, worrier from the womb,
a war-baby born, I'm told, with nails chewed down to the quick.

BACK TO THE LIGHT

They say it's better if a bruise comes out,
blooms like a flat blue rose. But some sink in
to be covered with layer on layer of skin,

tree-bark hiding the tell-tale rings of history.
That's why the dead fade slowly:
they peel inwards, are stripped to a faint

smudged core, always just out of range,
hints in mirrors, purplish shadows pressed
behind the eye, half-felt, half-guessed.

Melting to dream: a bright corridor;
without thinking I push through double doors
letting the heavy glass swing back on a girl –

and it's my girl, my daughter – to hit her full
on the forehead. Above her eye a deep ink-stain
gathers and spreads like a blot. I can't return,

can't reach her; can't heal the hurt;
back to the light, I feel myself dissolve
in an acid-bath of gold.

SEA GLOSE

The wind japans the surface. Like a flower,
each point of contact biggens and is gone.
And when it rains the senses fold in four.
No sky, no sea – the whiteness is all one.
                           Alice Oswald: *Sea Sonnet*

As the pilot turns the plane for a second try
the whole watery island's laid out below
adrift in an icy sea. The wind's so high
the fragile cabin sways and shakes; the flow
of talk tails off and fear makes our mouths dry.
We land with a lurch feeling the engine's power
bend our bodies and force the craft to slow –
then the terminal's warmth, my family.
In the distance the ocean's shining blur:
the wind japans the surface like a flower.

A flower, an Arum lily, great-niece Lily
in a great big white-wool hooded cardie, you
are the one I crossed the Atlantic to see, newly
born and gorgeous, your eyes the darkest blue
of the sea in dreams, open wide and nearly
ready to smile – at me or the Welsh Dragon
your far-away first-cousin-once-removed
has sent (you can't tell us apart this early!)
Outside, snow falls on tarmac and paving-stone;
each point of contact biggens and is gone.

Arctic pack ice drifts in overnight
and traps the sealing-boats, rams them together
off the north-east coast. From Cape Spear the white
slob-sheet boils like porridge, snow-water boulders
float on the waves or are sculpted into bright
green castles or blue blancmanges along the shore.
Later the wind swings round and the ice-cream colours
vanish as if by magic; in random sunlight
trees are encased in glass, a *silver thaw*.
And when it rains the senses fold in four.

The island's held by the sea, an empty sea
(so many miles for the eagle to fly across);
on Florrie's deck it's the smaller birds we feed,
nuthatches come, red squirrels and a mouse.
Rebecca, Deborah, Lily, Grant and Cle
(and not forgetting the furry lime-green dragon),
I'll miss you all, the young ones' clapboard house,
Cle's bake-apple jam, the chat, the sea, the sea.
Waving goodbye; I'm going, going, gone.
No sky, no sea – the whiteness is all one.

JUST LOOKING

Same house, same garden
and all the other houses, gardens
I've ever known bedded
down here in geological layers,

the sandpit the cats took over,
the patch where we planted forests
of runner beans, strata
we can never see again –

and a robin's bobbing around
clicking, now in the walnut tree,
now by the quince that's out at last,
smelling like orange blossom.

By the wall the tree peony's in flower
for the first time, its white
crinkly-paper head, gold stamens
unwrapped like a present –

the robin's eyeing me close-up –
and on the aquilegia spiky petals
not quite formed are saying
Look at me, look at me.

FIGURES IN A LANDSCAPE

Out loud, emphatic, though still asleep he says,
'Parsifal; The Easter Hymn.' How little I know
of his inner life even after all these years,
as if we were creatures moving about in mist,
shapes with weight and form but featureless
and with only those gestures we all have in common,
our individuality wearing away
until we're smooth as a pebble, stripped as a bone.

What will we know, either of us, out there
in the old hum of the garden; who will we greet
among the monoliths? Unstill, neither from
nor towards, we'll be reabsorbed in the pattern.
And what will remain? A block of unworked stone,
a mud-stained coat hanging behind a door.

SONG

When I think of being in the mountains with you
it's not Tivoli – rich blues of olive and cypress,
grape hyacinths in the grass, groves
drowned in the haze of their own blue leaves –

that I want, but a black lake that wells up
high in a Welsh cwm, ravens overhead
heard but not seen, the love song
of their harsh voices calling

and like reaching down into the cold
of LLyn Y Fan Fach for pebbles, I grasp at words,
dark-coloured, hold them in my palm

and feel how heavy they are for their size,
how fine the grain: *quartz, jasper,*
basalt, basanite, touchstone.

STONE LANTERNS

We tread with care; the steps are slippery,
the long staircase overhung by trees,
dusky even at noon.

The stone lanterns are blunted, effaced,
whatever names they had
long forgotten,

small cavities empty of oil
or candle; but even lampless
their nimbus shines.

Numberless feet have worn away these treads;
we hear sandals shuffling
where our boots follow

and it seems only right
that light should come from these stones,
be held there like heat.

VOICES

Love's in the air, or maybe in the grass
        of the orchard where we walk with Flora and Huw
choosing trees for their new garden, past each
        variety with its twin by its side, repetition
caressing the mind as if this is all there is

and while I watch wind ruffle the leaves, I'm thinking
        of Flora and a presence behind her I can't name,
not 'soul' or 'spirit', but a word more akin to 'solid'
        or 'true', and feel that old need to know
where love goes once we're outside time

remembering a bay, waves breasting the shore
        where I speak to my mother, whose voice I'll never hear
but who always listens, with the noise of the sea
        going on and on, the spray falling, and I wonder
when I leave time if my daughter will talk to me.

GHAZAL: OF LOVE

If I die will I leave you bereft of love?
Will you blame me, my love, for the theft of love?

'All lost, nothing lost': so Stendhal wrote;
we're found and held in the deepest cleft of love.

No sense of direction? Never mind!
Together, we're the right and the left of love.

Let go the string and soul would float off
but for earth's ballast, the bulk and heft of love.

You pull one way, I pull the other:
Lachlan, Mary in the warp and weft of love.

IN THE HUT OF FALLEN PERSIMMONS

Why should I – loving sunlight as I do –
long tonight to creep into your shadowy hut
that's overhung with branches and sit, quiet,

breathing the musty smell of damp tatami
as weeds make patterns against the window-paper
and rain drips ceaselessly from the roof?

BONNARD TO MARTHE

Glimpsed through the half-open door
or the crack of the hinge-gap
I catch the room re-arranging itself,
gathering around an empty space,

the crimson roses posed on the mat
which rests by the bath,
your underwater legs shimmering
where wet skin meets colour:

the optic nerve trembles.
It's looking askew that triggers it.
In front of the blank canvas
I see from the corner of my eye

how, just visible through the steam
at the far side of the bathroom,
soft light ruffling the white curtain,
I'm drawing my mirror image

while watching from the doorway
the intimacy of our solitudes.
Every time I see you
it's like entering a room suddenly.

BEAUTY

steps from the bath,
her face light and smooth
as a papier-mâché mask.

Dressed skin-tight
in skin, she disposes her limbs
precisely.

The moon arrives on cue
floating above
the scrape and click of bamboo.

Her breasts have bloomed, nipples
like small red flowers,
crushed camellia petals.

Light through the paper window
underscores each
with a strip of puckered shadow.

The one flaw that art
needs for perfection: a bruise
worn like a jewel at her throat.

ROOMS

That little dog with her paws on the table
   looks loved. Her head has been smoothed to a dome
by stroking; she presses against an arm, silky ears limp,
and snuffs the faint scent of coffee.
   The red check tablecloth is home
for her eye

and mine, the loose criss-cross weave vivid as paint
   on a brush, alive as the green chenille
which a child who sits at a table, long ago, riffles
as she reads, exploring its spring
   and texture that moves like muscle
under fur.

I haunt these remembered rooms and they give me
   the threads I follow, so I wish I knew
why at night I creep into a close-fitting cave and dream
in the colours of classroom ink,
   a spectrum from watery-eyed blue
to deep bruise.

JAR

In Lucy Rie's studio
there might be white dust
and the earth-smell of clay
covered with damp white cloths
but I can't tell:
it's a black and white photo
where everything's white.

And although she's old
propped up inside
her stiff white trouser suit
she's at least two hundred years younger
than the jar that rests beside her
on a rucked jumble of dust-sheets
like a lop-sided full moon.

The jar's faint whiteness highlights
her forehead and cheekbones
with its bleached moonstrings,
the same that drew me to the gallery
like a fish on a line, reeled me in
to a glass case, the jar's new home.
I want the pale glow to fall on me.

Now it casts its moon-shadow
on Lucy's still-life photo.
I think of her reading the blind face
like Braille, her fingers translating
all the knots and rubs in its skin
as she retraces the trail of an old Korean
who shaped his pot and gave it a name.

A survivor, it's gone through fire,
risen from ashes and bone-shards
to float, nameless, into our air.
At night it comes into its own.
I lie awake imagining it
pour a matt porcelain light into the room,
balance its bulge, its weight, beside me.

It speaks for itself in whispers
from mineral depths
promising something beyond heat
and worked clay, a patina
smoothed by dead hands, and I rest my cheek
on its warmth, feel its gravity-pull
as if it proved the afterlife of things.

NOCTURNE

In my house are stones, pots made of clay
and cloth dyed with leaf-sap and mud

but at night I think blue: lobsters
with blackish-blue claws, blotched, and an inky sea

that could be mackerel, a shoal feeding
just below the surface, swerving their sharp faces

to the horizon, silver on them as they turn
and shimmer like a skim of oil on small ripples.

Dream is an underwater where what's closed opens,
sea-anemones uncurl, weeds lift towards the light

and when the moon plays blue on the sea's surface,
more to be seen in reflections than in things.

IN GIORGIO MORANDI'S STUDIO

All is as you left it, but removed,
one piece at a time, to a windowless space.
Obsolete phone numbers pencilled on a wall,

a trilby hat, a paint-spattered jacket:
the vessels alone are purged of association
over-painted white, their history gone.

Dust is at home, but dust was always at home
and settled on your dear familiars:
you touched them all, arranged them into groups,

bottles, jars and humble kitchen things
and watched them form their mute relationships.
They seemed immune from time and change, stoic

collaborators in your lifetime's work.
Bric-a-brac now, they huddle round the easel
and only on canvas tremble into breath.

VASO DI FIORI

After Georgio Morandi

His memories of flowers, and ours
too, you pinkest of pink roses
in your plain white vase, with your heads

of wax or silk turned this way and that.
You accept your immobility;
no slightest breeze will stir your petals.

Earth colours the air around you
in shades of olive and ochre; your tone
also comes from earth, from *terra rossa,*

a red earth long unobtainable
which mixed with white gives a beautiful pink
such as one sees in the ancient frescoes.

Your dust has a familiar musty scent,
attar of what's left when flowers fade.
Poor naked roses confronting us

with intimacy, empty of meaning
unless we return that gaze; then, indeed,
you're saturated with suggestion.

MORANDI'S WALL

Side by side, the face in the mirror
takes on the lustre of late roses
in a vase on the mantelpiece: pinks
and reds, woman and roses, roses
and reflection, petals on marble.

These few roses, a face, a mirror –
in their shared moment a connection
is made, ambiguous but yet filled
with the resonance of simple things.
Outlines waver and nothing stands still.

In a street warmed by a quiet sun
an artist's blank yellow-ochre wall
reaches out suffused with feeling, proof
of what endures. O, let it be true
that *what will survive of us is love.*

PIAZZA DI SPAGNA, JANUARY 1821

As each candle fails, the next lights.
They're linked by a cotton thread; his eyes
follow the spark, a spot of fire
that feels like heat. Fairy lamplighters.

He listens to something filling, draining
away. In the piazza, the stone
boat flounders in the water, about
to sink. Its weight heavy on his chest.

Once there were words, doorways to wide
rooms he could move around in, the shape
of a poem that was a place to live,
a space to breathe easily in,

and he dreams long colonnades
of airy columns, and he's running
through them, their rhythms of light and shade,
and a sudden glimpse of smoke-pink cloud.

Now his room's in a frame, like sky
and trees reflected in a mirror at strange
intimate angles, somewhere empty
other people live, afterwards.

THE ARTIST

Not for him the old way, the calm Madonnas;
   his paint must be agitated like water in wind.
And he breaks the surface, roughens it,

   knows he must work fast to create breath
with a dry brush, expose the coarse weave.
   Three rapid strokes will do for splinters,

a fore-grounded blanket, then the plunge
   at an angle into the lazar-house
where the living, their sores running,

   and the dead are tended. Everywhere
racked men and women, animals, too,
   reach out in pain; a dog rests its head

between its paws. By the pool's troubled waters
   the sufferers call – Heal me! Heal me! –
or support a neighbour, beckoning to draw

   the healer's eye towards the more afflicted.
One springs up, cured, filling more than his space,
   his mattress flung over his shoulder.

Energy streams from the healer;
   his shadow falls on the sick as he moves
among them, almost lost in the crowd.

GHAZAL: IN THE DARK

Time's slipped its leash and is running wild in the dark.
Why must I feel like a frightened child in the dark?

'If you grow used to death he'll be your friend.' Never!
He's my enemy and most reviled in the dark.

Dreaming heads of meadowsweet, cream-tufted thistle –
but when sleep's denied there's nothing mild in the dark.

Constellations seed the sky, too many to count,
night's candles, flame and breath reconciled in the dark.

How high that voice – in Purcell's *Music for a While* –
holds me close with all my fears beguiled in the dark.

Now Cassiopeia's *W* is an *M*,
Mary's starry initial profiled in the dark.

GHAZAL

i.m. HV

Rainclouds have no colour of their own;
I want to write this wet on wet, like paint.

She craves colour and plunges into blue
deep as she can; yellow's out of reach.

Absence is white. White sheets and pillows,
a white nightdress. White the colour of mourning.

Everything's fragile now. In slow motion
the body's structures – its walls and towers – subside.

The flow of life's contained in a single line:
she holds one end and I hold the other.

Such zest as she tells of dawn on a mountain ridge,
it colours her cheek. We hardly hear her voice.

No-one knows the first breath, or the last.
The noise of rain arrives before the rain.

Her head's above the clouds and the air's so thin
I can hardly breathe, let alone say goodbye.

SKINS

An impossible balancing act
like walking on water –
low purplish rainclouds
weighted with their own wetness
and cumulonimbus, bright as icing sugar,
skim the skin delicately –
a glaze of transparent colour
floated on the river's blankness.

From dark streets
lighted rooms are pools:
fin up through their golden depths
like a shadowy carp, to break the surface
with a splash
and gasping mouth.

In a wide puddle
watch the moon
biting the sun.

Look through a train window
as night silvers the glass;
trees and flooded fields melt
to a face, a stare.

CELLS

The shape and size of a hand,
a mitten, dirty-white, grey-stone
colour, edged with a seam.
I couldn't see it at first,

hadn't noticed the bees
swarm in the half-dead plum tree.
'Lucky,' my neighbour says, pointing
to where they've left this mitt

hanging down from a twig,
its double layer of six-sided cells
perfect, intact and empty,
a honeyless comb.

It breaks clean from its cleft
and I hold it up to the light,
seeing my fingers spread out
in shadowy X-ray, transparent

behind its thick screen. Lucky bees,
I think, to build their hive
invisible among leaves and fruit,
then fly off, abandoning

this waxy hand I'm holding now
in mine, surprised how little
it weighs, how exactly it fits
between my palms, like a prayer.

THE SMILE

'I'd just been out of the room to make her a cup of tea;
as I came back she looked up at me with a loving smile

all over her face. Do you understand what I'm saying? –
her whole face, when her right side had been paralysed for months!

What a beautiful smile, I said, as I moved towards her.
What flashed through my mind was the incredible thought – she's cured! –

although I knew she wasn't. The next day a second stroke
destroyed her mind completely and she never spoke again,

didn't recognise me through all those weeks before she died.
Well, despite the bad weather, as it's Easter Day I thought

I'd go to church this morning, the first time in twenty years,
pushed my shopping trolley through the snow so I wouldn't slip.

But nothing helps me to account for that wonderful smile.
I can't make any sense of it, my dear; see if you can.'

IN THE WOOD

As we round the corner into the shallow valley
the leaves flash in the sun, though the coppice
is very black on either side of the path

and something fills the vista, a creature
larger than life, back-lit, in perfect close-up
as we look at him and he looks at us.

It's a shock; we're seeing what Pisanello paints
in the startled exchange between St Eustace
and the miraculous stag with Christ on the cross

in its antlers. Our stag has red-brown flanks
and seems to float above the woodland floor
in a deep silence – but whether it was silent

before or after we can't remember. He carries
his antlers like something precious balanced
on his head as he shifts and turns, poises

his hooves and is gone, up an invisible track
that cuts a sliver through tangled oak and yew.
And if I'd been alone I might have thought

I'd imagined it in this uneven light,
that the stag's too beautiful to be true, a vision
without a message, but you've seen him too,

and we search together for the path he took
while I keep a look-out, turning again and again,
half-fearing, half-expecting he's behind us.

NIGHT-WATCH

In a city, when a fox thinks
   itself alone as it slips along
in its own shadow, there are always

   eyes sleepless at windows watching
night's transformations. Here,
   in the open, I share the dark with

whatever's making that loud scuffling
   in the undergrowth; wearing black
I'm invisible and could disappear

   through the hedge or under the root
of a fallen tree. Further off,
   tawny owls swing their sound-lassos

and hold the wood, the silent birds,
   the stars and other night-watchers
fast within their echoing orbit.

TULIPS

When it's night a woman visits me; she walks stiffly across the bedroom, round the foot of the bed, not meeting my eyes. I say, 'Mother.' She doesn't resemble my mother at all. I can see the shape of her bones under the nothing-coloured dress: long white arms with jutting elbows, bird-legs that could be snapped with a finger-flick. I reach out. Something moves, the vase tips and breaks. Now the table is wet, the petals bloody. I think I'm dreaming my mother's dream.

SYBIL

after a painting by Marie-Louise von Motesiczky

The dressmaker worships the hem
with bright steel pins, crouching.
Even undressed, you're covered:
satin slip held by frail straps,
white skirt of an evening dress
and coral beads – light, hard –
floating on your fine shimmer.
'Such beautiful skin tone,' she says
through the pins, 'like pearl.'

In the hot, close room the dummy
wears a hooped cage, empty.
You hear the dressmaker's gold ring
click, click, as she folds and tucks,
circling your ankles, obeisant,
in your head a dry cranium click
and the scorched smell from the iron.
At full stretch you fill the void,
rigid, eyes like dark windows

to time's windswept tunnel where you scroll
through horrors, here in her room,
feel your flesh flow like lava
through the cool folds of the dress, and see
the mirror in its noose, dust falling
on clothes, shoes, twisted gold,
torn shreds pale on the floor.
Your skin in her hands, both bearing
the intolerable weight of compacted ash.

PRAYER

Day zero and once again
I'm swimming up through the thick dark silt
of anaesthetic

towards the light, but this time
someone's sobbing in great pent-up gasps
that make me angry

because no-one should cry here,
not like that, in front of the others,
and there's a kind voice

saying over and over,
'Don't cry,' which is intolerable
so I brace, push hard,

elbow my way to the top
and break the surface at last, chest tight,
face wet, throat rasping,

to hear the voice murmuring
softly in my ear, 'Don't cry, Mary,
there's no need to cry.'

SEASALTER

The sky lays its deep blue right over
the expanse of wet mud
at the lowest tide

as if it can't escape
its own self, that insistent intruder,
and the old piece of timber

that made a defence against the sea
is ruined on the foreshore
like a beam in the eye, splinter in the finger.

More and more what matters
is the blue's unburning centre,

happiness or grief tacked on
like frippery, a useless distraction.

WHAT THE WATERS BRING FORTH

In autumn salmon come home
knowing it's right to nose through shallows,

to leap with a mid-air twist
then rest, torpid, in clear brown waters.

At sea waves rise up on a breath
of green while inland streams invite

spotted trout to swim headlong
against the current, force equalling

force so that they hover
trembling above the gravel and spawn

in a tail-flicking spasm.
Our first watery home's the womb

with its other heartbeat and voice,
a mother's strange, familiar whale-hum:

mind doesn't remember but body
does at night, curled, one foot

resting on the other heel
or heel fitting snug into instep,

seeing through closed lids
ponds that mirror a wilderness,

the beauty of smooth, of salt,
of worm-casts and what is embedded.

INSIDE THE BRIGHTNESS OF RED

Mid-August, cold and grey-sodden; even
the Mexican sunflowers and the yellowy-green
of not yet fully ripened quinces are mute.

I've been protected so far by numb disbelief
as if this disease belongs to somebody else;
I'm a bit afraid and lonely, stepped back from life.

Later we leave a room, a voice that speaks
of drugs, the possibility of remission
and wander the streets side by side, speechless.

I feel your unhappiness seep into my ribs.
In the café are trays of red-gold peaches,
wooden tables, solid stools and benches;

the coffee smells of freshly-roasted beans,
the carrot cake's flecked with orange, crusted on top,
as if the world's set right, all as it should be.

But when I think of the dead – not as dead –
but as they were when alive or what they wrote
I know that all we can keep is their underlight.

*

I'm not heart-broken; that the cancer's come back
is natural but it makes me want to ask
what Heaven would be like if we could choose.

A scarlet boat-hull, blue-grey mud: the colours
on Oare Marsh today are so spacious,
and have such depth they're like lighted rooms

we could go into. Among the long-stemmed reeds
birds I've never seen before are hidden
in silky fronds then swing down to feed.

And if I want all this to last for ever,
never to end, it's not that I want to be
outside, merely a passive looker-on –

I want to be inside the brightness of red,
blow with the salty wind and feel the mud
press and ooze around an egret's foot;

more than that, to be conscious, to understand
what it is to be these things as only a god
can know. And yet I'm certain this isn't a good

answer to my question. Time to come down
to earth where we both still live, to what remains,
to finish our walk and watch the bearded tits

flit among the creamy-tasselled seed-heads;
but when I think of you left alone –
if it has to be – then, yes, I'm heart-broken.

BLUE MATERIAL

In the sun, wood-anemones are opening;
they have a strange blue aura, not the blueish-
pink on the underside of the petals, more
as if a shadow's just passed that's never there
when you look. It could be the breath of bluebells
half-showing in bud, or the far deeper tinge
violets weave through the wood-anemones' stars.
The ground is draped with this unravelled fabric.

I've made my will and thrown out all the old clothes
I don't wear, eight bags for the charity shop.
The cupboards and drawers are left almost empty.
I've listed my jewellery – the best pieces,
lapis, sapphire – and the friends who might like them.
And even a garment's hem can work a cure.

WILD GARLIC

Allium ursinum, ramson, sometimes ransom,
Old English *hramsa*: all Northern Europe
has a name for wild garlic, that startling white,
its pungency. Pick and they quickly fade
but in the mass – and what mass! – overwhelming.
In Cornwall they form thick banks along the lanes
and fill damp woods, making me long to be
propped on beds of amaranth and moly –

and truly I find they're magic: the moly-garlic
Hermes gave Odysseus to protect him.
Now hostage to fortune, how willingly
I'd pay a king's ransom – in ramsons, of course,
whole armfuls of them, a wild cornucopia –
for the smallest chance of release, remission.

VISITATION

In the garden a young woodpecker
is eating birdseed; he stretches from the branch
or hangs upside-down from the feeder
edging the seeds out with his pointed beak.
Later he pecks among the husks on the grass
and visits the walnut-tree like a blessing
bestowed without thought or motive, a free gift.

At night I summon him inside my head;
he opens his chequered wings, angelic,
and his crimson cap distracts me from fear.

JOURNEY ACROSS THE TUNDRA

I'm dreaming burnt bones, entrails, smoke.
Above, a huge bird with deep-set unmoving eyes
splays its claws, waiting for flesh;

he won't be satisfied until I've cried.
Everyone who asks here must sink to the lowest depth.
You may be paralysed; time will stop.

The yellow circle of his stare meets mine,
the dark throat quivers;
he made me ask the question that broke me.

My companion, husband, lover,
always so quiet and self-disciplined,
whom I've never seen in tears, is distraught,

his hair, each individual strand, red
and sharp, a fox's coat, sparking, glittering,
while I turn to granite, unable to feel.

Self, memory: the containing walls
crumble apart, the narrative gone.
We plunge down into cold underground halls

where what cuts against us is dirt, roots
scraping our sides, pushing under finger-nails.
How small and concentrated the carrion bird is

on his next appearance, half-size as if wrapped
in dry horse-chestnut leaves, like a cape;
rat-runs into the cave-mouth are filled

with ancient debris, meaningless.
Everyone who asks here must sink to the lowest depth.
All who visit here will leave crying.

*

In the half-light shamans fly across the space
or invoke their spirits in corners. What words
are these I speak? Whose dream am I part of?

I think they will section me, lock me away
for ever. The limbs that are stretched on a slab,
exposed, unable to move, are mine.

Dark twin doors swing close behind me.
A needle is scratched on my hand,
a formula intoned.

*

My heart which was dark as raven is now white as mist.

The mountains open and the singer passes through.
We hear his deep contentment, the swirling harmonics
above the secret language of the epic Altai poem,

his growling throat-singing. Footsteps reverberate
from golden stones. *The grey-headed cuckoo knows
who has a happy fortune, mourns the unhappy.*

Tall trees bloom with prayer-flowers
and long-robed priests walk among them;
each blossom's mouth is filled with perfume.

At Dinefwr the Roman sacrificial cattle,
creamy white, browse quietly, recall their past.
Horses' breath mingles in the moonlight.

*

I'm searching for something to fill this absence
I've lived with all my life,
that isn't about prayer but is a prayer

sent out into the void that the body
may be able to renew and heal itself
and the small individual life, its repetitions

and patterns may move within the patterns
of the natural world; that my grandson Emyr Ceidrych
may be a path to a future unimaginable to me,

praising the day we found the source of the stream
that gives him his middle name; the capstone
and the water welling up, pure and cold,

and the wind like a fanfare through the holly trees,
untroubling the berries, orange and unripe,
until winter comes and the berries redden.

ON THE BLACK MOUNTAIN

Above the noise of the wind larks are singing –
the same outpouring you heard, Rosenberg,
as you returned stubbornly from battle.

Love burns more fiercely with age,
fed by the longing to go on,
knowing what it is to be fragile,
its flame double, an outer heat
and an inner cone, cool, unmoving.

And if we could return to the mountain –
wouldn't these ground-nesting birds,
the skylarks, be singing overhead?

UN-NAMED

Turning back to look through an open door
I catch for an instant the desk,
the lamp, computer screen and phone,

the view from the window of elm-tree
and rickety fence, all reflected
in the glass of a picture-frame, familiar,

my study still, and utterly transformed,
drained dry and clear, unweighted.
Inviting. Oh, how inviting!

AFTERWORD

Mary MacRae was a poet of the lyric moment in all its facets: now turning to the past, the elsewhere, the 'world-when-I'm gone', now swinging back to the axis of the here and now, her lyric longing intensifying into praise and prayer. With an instinct for transcendence but also for accommodation, she let her poems alight – 'as birds do' – however briefly, before they flew again, leaving their after-image in mind and ear.

Drawn to the natural world, Mary's desire to look and see was so intense, her delight so child-like, that she could lose herself entirely, allow the self to step aside, the thing to speak for itself. Fearlessly honest, able to look things in the eye, she also revelled in the subtleties of peripheral vision – looking through door hinges, branches, paper windows, steam. She was receptive to positive and negative space, stars and interstellar spaces, whatever might be 'more to be seen in reflections than in things'. She was alive to the time for letting go – welcoming colour, but also whiteness in which all colours merge.

The world of Mary's poetry is a rounded world, where day balances night, reality/dreams, solace/fear, where the elements she most naturally swims in, air, earth, water, are balanced by the fragile fire, doubleflamed, of love. 'What happens to love after time?' she asks, delving into the interstices of time as well as space, where 'the noise of rain arrives before the rain'.

In the title poem of *Inside the Brightness of Red*, we hear her at her most direct: 'not that I want to be/outside, merely a passive looker-on –//I want to be inside the brightness of red…' and in the verbs that follow – *blow* with the wind, *feel* the mud, *to be conscious, to understand* – Mary's central vision, almost pantheistic, in which 'we'll be reabsorbed in the pattern' or 'become fragments in the dust particulate' comes wholly into view. We cannot read Mary without *becoming* her, so strong is her empathy with all living things, so intense her desire to be fully alive, so palpable her sense of mortality. This is the gift of her imagination: to *become* the object of her looking, be it bird, flower, light, shadow, and, in turn, to gift us with her poetry of transformation. Hers was a unifying vision which produced an extraordinarily coherent body of work, a true wedding of spiritual and material worlds and, unobtrusively, of form and content.

Because of the natural ease and grace of her diction, it would be easy to overlook Mary's versatile formal skills, employed in sonnets, syllabics (à la Marianne Moore), numerous stanzaic forms, but nowhere evidenced more forcefully than in her Glose here, inspired by Marilyn Hacker's examples, in which she pays homage to Alice Oswald, as in a previous Glose to Mary Oliver – a trinity of wonderful lyric poets, in whose company Mary, modest but not lacking in ambition, shyly holds her own. I do wish that she could have received more general acclaim for her considerable achievements during her lifetime. But she would have been proud, as we are for her, of this moving posthumous collection.

Mimi Khalvati